What is now proved was once only imagin'd.

WILLIAM BLAKE (1757–1827)
ENGLISH ARTIST AND POET

ISBN 1–56138–315–5

Cover photographs © Kathy Lynn
Cover design by Toby Schmidt
Interior design by Lili Schwartz
Interior illustrations by Gary Davis
Edited by Melissa Stein
Typography by Richard Conklin
Printed in the United States

This book may be ordered by mail from the publisher.
Please add $2.50 for postage and handling.
But try your bookstore first!

Running Press Book Publishers
125 South Twenty-second Street
Philadelphia, Pennsylvania 19103–4399

Dreams

A PERSONAL NOTEBOOK, WITH QUOTES AND ILLUSTRATIONS

RUNNING PRESS
PHILADELPHIA · LONDON

. . . Sleep hath its own world,
And a wide realm of wild reality. . . .

GEORGE GORDON, LORD BYRON (1788–1824)
ENGLISH POET

*Why does the eye see a thing more clearly in
dreams than the imagination when awake?*

In all of us, even in good men, there is a lawless, wild beast nature, which peers out in sleep.

SOCRATES (469–399 B.C.)
GREEK PHILOSOPHER

Dreaming permits each and every one of us to be quietly and safely insane every night of our lives.

WILLIAM DEMENT, B. 1928
AMERICAN PSYCHIATRIST

*Dreams are often most profound when they seem
most crazy.*

SIGMUND FREUD (1856–1939)
AUSTRIAN PSYCHIATRIST

I was not looking for my dreams to interpret my life, but rather for my life to interpret my dreams.

SUSAN SONTAG, B. 1933
AMERICAN WRITER

Dreams! my dreams are always disagreeable—mere confusions—losing my clothes and the like, nothing beautiful. The same dreams go on night after night for a long time. I am a <u>worse</u> man in my dreams than when awake—do cowardly acts, dreams of being tried for a crime.

THOMAS CARLYLE (1795–1881)
SCOTTISH ESSAYIST AND HISTORIAN

Dreams are caused by electrochemical signals darting helter-skelter around the brain, like untied balloons released in a room. The familiar expression "I had a dream" should probably be reversed: "A dream had me!"

EDWARD DOLNICK
20TH-CENTURY AMERICAN WRITER

He whose talk is of oxen will probably dream of oxen.

THOMAS DE QUINCEY (1785–1859)
ENGLISH WRITER

There have been times in my life when I have fallen asleep in tears; but in my dreams the most charming forms have come to console and to cheer me, and I have risen the next morning fresh and joyful.

JOHANN WOLFGANG VON GOETHE (1749–1832)
GERMAN POET

Not only is our power of imagination greater in our sleep than in our waking life, but the innate strivings for health and happiness often assert themselves in our sleep more forcefully than when we are awake.

ERICH FROMM (1900–1980)
AMERICAN PSYCHOANALYST

If we listen patiently to our dreams and the messages they contain . . . they will eventually lead us to health. . . . How much better to take advice from the other half of yourself than from another person.

ANN FARADAY, B. 1935
ENGLISH PSYCHOLOGIST

A person who dreams lives long.

FLORINDA DONNER
20TH-CENTURY BRITISH WRITER

Dreams may seem as fragile and floating as silk chiffon,
but they are nevertheless sturdy props for easing our way.

PATRICIA GARFIELD, B. 1955
AMERICAN PSYCHOLOGIST

We are asleep with compasses in our hands.

W. S. MERWIN, B. 1927
AMERICAN POET

The time that nature has ordained for us to consecrate to repose brings us, with sleep, an accessory more precious than sleep itself; that natural necessity becomes a source of enjoyment and we do not sleep merely to live, but to learn to live well.

SYNESIUS OF CYRENE (C. 370–413)
GREEK PRELATE AND PHILOSOPHER

Sleep takes off the costume of circumstance, arms us with terrible freedom, so that every will rushes to a deed. A skillful man reads his dreams for his self-knowledge; yet not the details but the quality.

RALPH WALDO EMERSON (1803–1882)
AMERICAN ESSAYIST AND POET

All that we see or seem
Is but a dream within a dream.

EDGAR ALLAN POE (1809–1849)
AMERICAN POET AND WRITER

In some ways, your dreams may speak a universal language, and therefore they belong not only to you but to a larger community. Others may find wisdom for themselves in your dream.

LOUIS M. SAVARY
20TH-CENTURY AMERICAN WRITER AND SCHOLAR

All human beings are also dream beings. Dreaming ties all mankind together.

JACK KEROUAC (1922–1969)
CANADIAN-BORN AMERICAN WRITER

Because dreams come from the unconscious, they share the same language of symbolism as art, myths, folklore, and religious ritual, which all spring from the imagination.

KAREN A. SIGNELL
20TH-CENTURY AMERICAN PSYCHOLOGIST AND WRITER

Even sleepers are workers and collaborators on what goes on in the universe.

HERACLITUS (C. 600–500 B.C.)
GREEK PHILOSOPHER

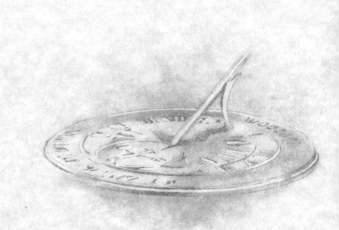

In our dreams we are the creators of a world where time and space, which limit all the activities of our body, have no power.

ERICH FROMM (1900–1980)
AMERICAN PSYCHOANALYST

One of the characteristics of the dream is that nothing surprises us in it.

JEAN COCTEAU (1889–1963)
FRENCH WRITER AND FILMMAKER

Our dreams are firsthand creations, rather than residues of waking life. We have the capacity for infinite creativity; at least while dreaming, we partake of the power of the immanent Spirit, the infinite Godhead that creates the cosmos.

GORDON GLOBUS
20TH-CENTURY AMERICAN PSYCHIATRIST AND WRITER

. . . every night, while replenishing our energy, for the next day, in deep sleep, we visit the Great Spaces of the mind; but, on waking up, they are forgotten.

GORDON ONSLOW-FORD, B. 1921
ENGLISH PAINTER

A moment's insight is sometimes worth a life's experience.

OLIVER WENDELL HOLMES (1809–1894)
AMERICAN PHYSICIAN AND WRITER

Man lives by imagination.

HAVELOCK ELLIS (1859–1939)
ENGLISH PHYSICIAN AND WRITER

If a little day-dreaming is dangerous, the cure for it is not to dream less but to dream more, to dream all the time.

MARCEL PROUST (1871–1922)
FRENCH WRITER

Imagination is more important than knowledge.

ALBERT EINSTEIN (1879–1955)
GERMAN-BORN AMERICAN SCIENTIST

There emerges from time to time in the creations and fabrics of the genius of dreams a depth and intimacy of emotion, a tenderness of feeling, a clarity of vision, a subtlety of observations, and a brilliance of wit such as we should never claim to have at our permanent command in our waking lives.

SIGMUND FREUD (1856–1939)
AUSTRIAN PSYCHIATRIST

There is a dream dreaming us.

A KALAHARI BUSHMAN,
QUOTED BY JOSEPH CAMPBELL

Imagination frames events unknown,
In wild, fantastic shapes of hideous ruin,
And what it fears creates.

HANNAH MORE (1745–1833)
ENGLISH WRITER AND REFORMER

Imagination is the eye of the soul.

. . .all that we call lives and souls, lie dreaming, dreaming, still; tossing like slumberers in their beds; the ever-rolling waves but made so by their restlessness.

HERMAN MELVILLE (1819–1891)
AMERICAN WRITER

Just as the waters of earth swell and recede, so our dreams change over time.

PATRICIA GARFIELD, B. 1955
AMERICAN PSYCHOLOGIST

A dream which is not understood is like a letter which is not opened.

THE TALMUD

. . . there is nothing lasting in any touch of the fabulous we experience outside sleep.

COLETTE (1873–1954)
FRENCH WRITER

What is life? A madness. What is life? An illusion, a shadow, a story. And the greatest good is little enough: for all life is a dream, and dreams themselves are only dreams.

PEDRO CALDERÓN DE LA BARCA (1600–1681)
SPANISH WRITER

Those who compared our life to a dream were right. . . .
We sleeping wake, and waking sleep.

MICHEL EYQUEM DE MONTAIGNE (1533–1592)
FRENCH ESSAYIST

Most of us today think of our dreams as odd episodes, as foreign as some strange ceremonial dance in Tibet. This results in the cutting off of an exceedingly great and significant portion of the self. We are then no longer able to use much of the wisdom and power of the unconscious.

ROLLO MAY, B. 1909
AMERICAN PSYCHOANALYST AND WRITER

I arise from dreams of thee
In the first sweet sleep of night. . .

PERCY BYSSHE SHELLEY (1792–1822)
ENGLISH POET

Here we are all, by day; by night, we're hurled
By dreams, each one into a several world.

ROBERT HERRICK (1591–1674)
ENGLISH POET

... *We are such stuff*
As dreams are made on, and our little life
Is rounded with a sleep.

WILLIAM SHAKESPEARE (1564–1616)
ENGLISH DRAMATIST AND POET

Take, if you must, this little bag of dreams,
Unloose the cord, and they will wrap you round.

WILLIAM BUTLER YEATS (1865–1939)
IRISH POET